the sand

3

Observe and Prompt

Word Recognition

- Ask the children where they think the girl is.
- How do the children think she might be feeling?

Walkthrough

The girl is building something.

What is she using? (*the spade*)

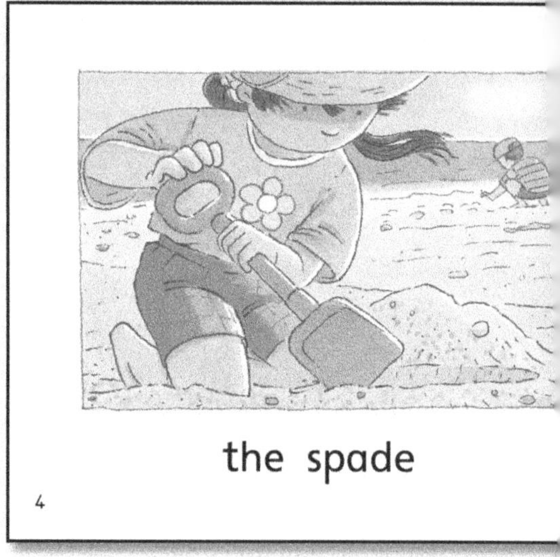

Observe and Prompt

Word Recognition

- The word 'spade' will not be decodable for the children at this stage. Ask them if they recognise the adjacent consonants – 'sp'. Then tell them this word, modelling the reading of it for them.

- If the children have difficulty with 'shells', ask them if they recognise the initial letters and sound – 'sh'. Then encourage them to blend all the sounds through the word.

4

Can you see what she is building?

What has the boy found? (*the shells*)

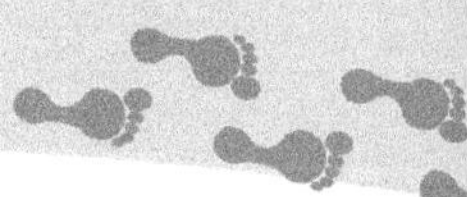

the shells

5

 **Observe and Prompt**

Language Comprehension

- Ask the children what the boy is looking at. Where is he?
- What do the children think the girl is using her spade for?
- What else do the children think might happen at the seaside?

Walkthrough

What has the boy found? (*the stick*)

What could he use it for?

the stick

6

● **Observe and Prompt**

Word Recognition

- If the children have difficulty with the word 'stick', ask them if they recognise the initial letter and sound – 's'. Then encourage them to blend the sounds from left to right, through the word.

- The word 'sandcastle' may not be decodable for the children at this stage. Tell them this word and model the reading of it for them.

Walkthrough

Were you right?

What did the children build? (*the sandcastle*)

the sandcastle

7

 **Observe and Prompt**

Language Comprehension

- Ask the children what the children in the story have made.
- How do they think the children are feeling?
- What do they think the children might say?

Walkthrough

What has happened? (*the sea has come in*)

Discuss the fact that the tide has come in and
the sea has covered the sandcastle.

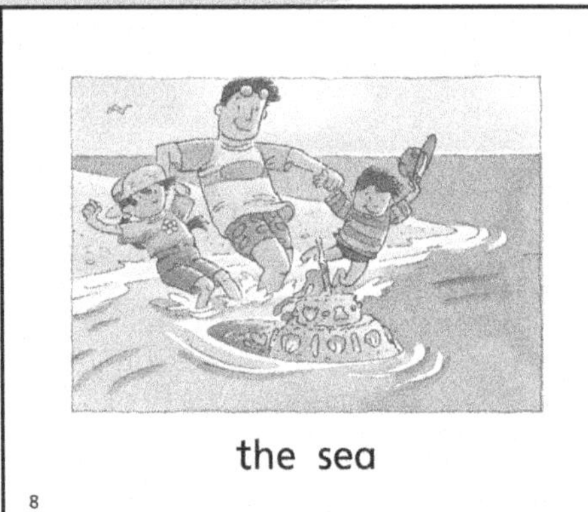

![Observe eye icon] **Observe and Prompt**

Word Recognition

- The word 'sea' may not be decodable for the children at
  this stage. Ask them if they recognise the initial letter and
  sound – 's'. Then tell them this word and model the reading
  of it for them.

Language Comprehension

- Check the children understand what has happened at the
  end of the story.